Sauce and Condiment Cookbook

The Best Homemade Sauces and Condiments Recipes to Complement Your Everyday Dishes

by Noah Wood

Copyright © 2022 by Noah Wood. All Rights Reserved.

⟨XXXXXXXXXXXXXXXXX⟩

Copyright License

Stop. What. You're. Doing. This isn't going to be a tiny fine print you'll never see because I'd much rather be honest and open with you about how much I value mine and my team's work. To be honest, I don't know if you will ever intend to reproduce, copy, distribute (etc.). This book with anyone, but just so we're on the same page, here goes:

You aren't allowed to make any print or electronic reproductions, sell, re-publish, or distribute this book in parts or as a whole unless you have express written consent from me or my team.

We have worked extremely hard on all of the content you'll find here, so please help us maintain it by not sharing it with other people. Other than that, please be careful when making our recipes! If you aren't sure how to carry out some steps, do some research before going any further, especially if it involves using a knife or an open flame. My team nor I take any responsibility for any of the interpretations given to our recipes. See you in the kitchen!

Table of Contents

Introduction 6

Uses 8

Types of Sauces 9

    1. Chili-Garlic Sauce 11

    2. Pesto 13

    3. Ketchup 15

    4. Hot Sauce 18

    5. Barbecue Sauce 20

    6. Hollandaise Sauce 22

    7. Teriyaki Sauce 24

    8. Honey-Mustard Sauce 26

    9. Arugula and Walnut Pesto 28

    10. Tzatziki Sauce 30

    11. Tartar Sauce 32

    12. Guacamole 34

    13. Cilantro and Mint Chutney 36

14. Gravy 38

15. Tonkatsu Sauce 40

16. Salsa Verde 42

17. Blue Cheese Dressing 44

18. Garlic Aioli 46

19. Marinara Sauce 48

20. Chinese Style Sesame Sauce 50

21. Franks Style Hot Sauce 52

22. Sweet Onion Sauce 54

23. Garlic and Chive Sauce 56

24. Mint and Peanut Thick Sauce 58

25. Asian Garlic Sauce 60

26. Balsamic Vinaigrette 62

27. Salted Caramel Sauce 64

28. Maple Dijon Sauce 66

29. Spicy Watermelon and Papaya Salsa 68

30. Baba Ghanoush 70

Conclusion 72

Afterthought 73

Biography 74

Introduction

Sauces are perfect to complement certain dishes and can make the best meals even tastier. Sauces are popular because this liquid or semi-cream condiment will improve flavor, moisture and visual appearance of your dishes.

Sauces can be completely liquid, foamy or semi-cream, but regardless the structure, they share one common effect; they improve almost any meal.

Certain dishes like pasta, barbecue or meat dishes are almost unthinkable without sauces. Besides savory dishes, sauces can be used as dessert condiments, so fruity sauces or chocolate-based sauces will perfectly complement sweet dishes like cakes or puddings.

Sauces have a long history and when something with such long history is still "king" among condiments, it must be really good.

When it comes to serving, sauces can be hot or cold, as part of a dish like pasta, or served on the side as a condiment.

Sauces are marvels on a table. It can enhance any dish – even a poorly prepared one – and will make any meal a great meal.

Uses

Sauces can impart moisture as well as flavor to food, unlike dry spice or flavor mixes. They can also provide contrast and balance to different dishes. For example, the tartness and lightness of a fruit coulis beautifully contrast with the heaviness and fat of a cheesecake, and the sweetness of British mint sauce balances the savor and depth of roast lamb. Sauces are often matched with dishes for visual appeal as well as for flavor. The bright, deep red of raspberry shows up wonderfully on the subtle cream color of cheesecake, and the clear green of mint sauce complements the rich brown and red colors of roast lamb. Chefs use sauces in squeeze bottles, pipettes, or even on the back of a spoon to make various appealing designs on their dishes, ranging from simple and classic to intricate and artistic.

While some sauces are served as toppings or side dishes, others are used in the cooking process to give flavor to the dish. Barbecue sauce is commonly used to baste barbecued meat for hours upon hours before the dish is completed. Worcestershire sauce and soy sauce are used by many cooks to give depth and complexity to soups and stews. Marinades can imbue all kinds of different meats with various flavors prior to cooking.

Types of Sauces

Some sauces are defined by one particular ingredient. A sauce is not a hot sauce if it does not contain chili peppers in some form. Balsamic vinaigrette must include grape must be as a primary or singular ingredient. Soy sauce is defined by the presence of fermented soybean paste. Herb sauce is always made from herbs and tomato sauce from tomatoes. Fruit sauce, unsurprisingly, must contain fruit.

Salsa generally contains tomatoes, onions, or chilies, but this sauce is usually defined by Latin American cultural origin rather than ingredients.

Sweet and sour sauce is categorized by flavors, not ingredients, and any sauce that primarily features sweet and sour flavors in roughly equal measures can be called "sweet and sour sauce".

Other sauces are defined by the dishes they have traditionally accompanied, such as BBQ sauce for Southern American barbecue, teriyaki sauce for Japanese teriyaki, sweet sauce for desserts, salad dressings for salads, and marinades for marinades. For the most part, however, these sauces are not limited by their traditional uses and can be used effectively and deliciously in a wide variety of other dishes, with the exception of marinades.

Lastly, sauces such as Worcestershire sauce and white sauce are specifically associated with a particular recipe and cooking process.

Sauces can be cooked, such as white (béchamel) sauce, or uncooked, like pesto. Many herb sauces, Latin American salsas, and salad dressings are served cold, whereas other sauces such as tomato-based pasta sauce and teriyaki sauce, are generally served warm. Most sauces can be served on the side of dishes or served as part of the dish itself. They can vary in texture from chunky to silky smooth, and in consistency from as thick as dessert custard, to as thin and runny as tabasco sauce or light soy sauce, depending on their intended uses within the larger dish.

1. Chili-Garlic Sauce

One of the best things to pair your noodle soups and dumplings with is this very Asian sauce. It was meant to give Sriracha a run for its money and rightfully so. A serving of the side sauce could easily make your meals a tad more delightful with a significant kick.

Serving Size: 1 cup

Preparation Time: 12 minutes

Ingredients:

- 20 red chili peppers, chopped
- 2 garlic heads, peeled and lightly roasted
- 2 shallots, finely minced
- 3 tablespoons white vinegar
- 2 tablespoons peanut oil
- 1 teaspoon fish sauce
- 1 tablespoon sugar
- Salt to taste

Instructions:

Place chilies, roasted garlic, vinegar, sugar, and salt in a blender or food processor and pulse to a paste.

Heat oil in your pan on medium low and sauté the shallots for about 2 minutes.

Stir in blended chili-garlic paste, plus fish sauce. Adjust seasoning as needed.

2. Pesto

Pesto has a lot of uses. Use it as a dipping sauce for your chips or as a spread on your bread. Use it also to enhance the flavor of your meat or fish dinner. You can even toss some into some cooked pasta, and you will have a meal in an instant. That's why it is pretty clever to have a jar of pesto at home. Are you ready for some action? We're going to make this basic fresh basil pesto!

Serving Size: 2 cups

Preparation Time: 15 minutes

Ingredients:

- 2 tablespoons pine nuts
- 2 garlic cloves
- ½ cup extra-virgin olive oil
- ½ cup parmesan cheese, freshly grated
- 2 cups fresh basil leaves

Instructions:

Mince basil, garlic, and nuts in a food processor and pulse until finely minced.

Gently pour in oil and continue to pulse slowly until well mixed.

Stir in cheese and pulse again for about 5 seconds.

Serve and enjoy!

3. Ketchup

You don't need to always buy bottled ketchup to use at home. You can make this tomato ketchup recipe, and in no time, you will have a flavorful dipping sauce ready for your fried chicken, sausages, chunky chips, burgers, and more! It keeps well in the fridge for a long so you should not be afraid about making a good batch!

Serving Size: 2 ¾ cups

Preparation Time: 55 minutes

Ingredients:

- 1 32-ounce can whole tomatoes
- 1 onion, chopped
- 4 garlic cloves, chopped
- 1 tablespoon tomato paste
- ½ cup cider vinegar
- 2 tablespoons vegetable oil
- ½ teaspoon paprika
- ¼ teaspoon ground allspice
- ¼ teaspoon cinnamon
- 1 teaspoon chili powder
- ½ cup brown sugar
- ¼ teaspoon salt
- ½ teaspoon ground black pepper

Instructions:

Pour the contents of the can of whole tomatoes (including the juices) in a blender or food processor and pulse until smooth. Set aside.

Meanwhile, heat oil in a pan and sauté onions and garlic until fragrant.

Sprinkle with salt and pepper and the rest of the spices and continue stirring for about 8 minutes.

Add pureed tomatoes plus tomato paste, vinegar, and sugar.

Let it simmer for around 45 minutes or 'til smooth and thick, stirring occasionally.

Once the ketchup has completely cooled, pour back into the food processor and pulse until really smooth.

Serve after chilling for at least 2 hours.

4. Hot Sauce

If you are somewhat of a hot sauce person, you should try making this concoction that's in a league of its own. It will certainly give the once reliable Sriracha a run for its money with its fresh flavor and authentic spiciness. What's even more amazing is that you can easily adjust the level of spiciness according to your liking by mixing medium hot to super-hot chili varieties.

Serving Size: 2 ½ cups

Preparation Time: 20 minutes

Ingredients:

- 1 pound fresh red chilies, stemmed
- 2 cups distilled white vinegar
- 3 tablespoons kosher salt

Instructions:

Place the chilies and salt in a food processor and pulse until finely minced, occasionally stopping to scrape down the sides.

Transfer to a tight lid glass jar and set in a cool and dry place and leave it for about 2 days. After 2 days, stir in vinegar, cover, and set aside for another 5 days or until the flavors develop.

Strain the liquid to another bottle using a fine mesh, discarding the solids.

Shake well before using.

5. Barbecue Sauce

A good barbecue sauce should be tangy, smoky, and rich - just like this one. Serve in burgers, ribs or any barbecue beef, lamb or even chicken. Pour in a sterilized bottle and you can refrigerate it for up to two weeks.

Serving Size: 2 ½ cups

Preparation Time: 25 minutes

Ingredients:

- ¾ cup of passata
- 6 ½ tablespoons maple syrup
- 3 tablespoons Worcestershire sauce
- 3 ½ tablespoons black treacle
- 3 ½ tablespoons tomato ketchup
- 3 ½ tablespoons malt vinegar
- 1 tablespoon mustard
- 1 teaspoon garlic powder
- Pinch of paprika
- Salt and pepper

Instructions:

Put the passata, maple syrup and black treacle in a saucepan.

Add the tomato ketchup, malt vinegar and Worcestershire sauce.

Add the mustard, garlic powder, paprika and season.

Bring to the boiling stage and simmer gently for 10 to 15 minutes.

As soon as it is reduced slightly and thickened and serve it.

6. Hollandaise Sauce

What's an Eggs Benedict without a delicious hollandaise sauce to match? If only for such a delightful brunch staple, it is definitely worth making the classic on your own, even when a bottled variety is easily reachable at grocery stores. Apart from an Eggs Benedict, you can also enjoy it as a dipping sauce for your blanched veggie and fish recipes.

Serving Size: 1 cup

Preparation Time: 25 minutes

Ingredients:

- 3 egg yolks
- ¼ pound unsalted butter, sliced into chunks and divided
- ½ cup white wine, divided
- 1 tablespoon white vinegar
- 1 tablespoon fresh lemon juice
- 4 peppercorns
- Salt and pepper to taste

Instructions:

Combine egg yolks and freshly squeezed lemon juice in a saucepan and heat on medium low. Whisk vigorously until doubled in volume and long before the yolk starts to curdle.

Stir in half of the butter and the wine and continue stirring until the butter has melted.

Continue whisking with the remaining butter and wine.

Pour in vinegar, then sprinkle with peppercorns, salt, and ground pepper.

Serve warm.

7. Teriyaki Sauce

So, you already have your barbecue sauce and Tonkatsu sauce. What more would you need this teriyaki sauce for? Well, it's for those who appreciate the difference it makes, especially when it is used as a glaze for your chicken wings, salmon, pork, and others. The great thing about this sauce recipe is that it can keep well in the fridge for up to 3 weeks as long as it is stored properly.

Serving Size: 1 cup

Preparation Time: 10 minutes

Ingredients:

- 1 teaspoon ginger, minced
- 2 garlic cloves, finely minced
- ½ cup fresh orange juice
- ⅓ cup soy sauce
- ½ cup water
- 3 tablespoons brown sugar
- 2 tablespoons cornstarch, dissolved in
- 2 tablespoons water

Instructions:

Stir together ginger, garlic, orange juice, water, soy sauce, and sugar in a pan and simmer on medium low until the sugar has dissolved.

Pour in cornstarch slurry and continue to simmer for another 5 minutes or so until the sauce is thick and smooth.

Serve and enjoy with your favorite dishes or store in a jar and keep chilled.

8. Honey-Mustard Sauce

This sauce can be used for a lot of things. You may utilize it as a dipping sauce for your chips, bread and biscuits. You may also flavor up your fried treats with it. Best of all, you can drizzle it into your salads or simply serve it with cut up veggies and fruit for a healthy finger food experience.

Serving Size: 1 cup

Preparation Time: 5 minutes

Ingredients:

- ½ cup mustard, stone-ground
- ¼ cup honey
- ¼ cup rice vinegar

Instructions:

Whisk all the ingredients in your bowl 'til well blended.

Transfer to a jar with a tight lid and keep refrigerated until ready to use.

9. Arugula and Walnut Pesto

Unlike the classic basil pesto, this one has some common ingredients that are easy to find all year round. Also, its taste is milder than the basil version and earthier, but it works great with pasta or in sandwiches, being just as healthy as the classic one.

Serving Size: 1 cup

Preparation Time: 7 minutes

Ingredients:

- 3 cups arugula leaves
- 2 garlic cloves
- 4 tablespoons olive oil
- 4 ounces walnuts, slightly toasted
- 2 ounces grated Parmesan cheese
- salt, pepper to taste

Instructions:

Put the arugula leaves, garlic and walnuts in a food processor or blender and pulse a few times until smooth.

Gradually pour in the olive oil, then stir in the Parmesan and adjust the taste with salt and pepper.

Use immediately or you may keep it in a jar in the fridge for 3-4 days.

10. Tzatziki Sauce

This sauce is a classic one, having Greek origins. It only uses yogurt, cucumber, garlic and dill, but it has such a fresh taste, and it works great with any dish, from steaks to sandwiches and fries.

Serving Size: 1 cup

Preparation Time: 5 minutes

Ingredients:

- 1 cup Greek style yogurt
- 1 tablespoon fresh chopped dill
- 1 cucumber, peeled and grated
- 2 garlic cloves, minced
- salt, pepper
- 1 tablespoon olive oil

Instructions:

Put the yogurt in a bowl. Take your grated cucumber and squeeze out the liquid with your hands.

Stir the cucumber in the yogurt, followed by the dill, garlic, olive oil and a pinch of salt and pepper.

Serve immediately or keep it in your fridge, but not for more than 1 day.

11. Tartar Sauce

Fish and Fries will not be such a pleasurable experience if it does not come with a delicious tartar sauce that is tangy and quite spicy. It has a lot of flavors, yet it does take away the spotlight from the main dishes. Although there is a store-bought version of it that you can go-to anytime, it is still much better if you could pull the rugs for the recipe so you can enjoy a healthier and tailored-to-your-taste version when you make your fish sticks. You may also use it for your salads and other food that needs dunking to some delicious sauces.

Serving Size: 1 ½ cups

Preparation Time: 15 minutes

Ingredients:

- 1 tablespoon parsley, finely chopped
- 2 tablespoons onion, finely chopped
- 1 cup mayonnaise
- 1 cup dill pickles, finely chopped
- ¼ teaspoon freshly ground black pepper
- 1 teaspoon sugar
- 1 teaspoon lemon juice

Instructions:

Place the ingredients in a bowl and stir until well combined.

Cover with a sheet of plastic wrap or transfer to a tightly lidded jar and keep refrigerated until ready to use.

12. Guacamole

Guacamole is the heart of an enjoyable Mexican nachos experience. But with its creamy, fresh, and super delicious character, you can pair it with a lot of things as well. You can use it as a dipping sauce for other things or spread it on your toasts, sandwiches and whatnots.

Serving Size: 1 cup

Preparation Time: 10 minutes

Ingredients:

- 3 avocados, peeled, seeded, and mashed
- 2 Roma tomatoes, diced
- ½ onion, finely diced
- 2 garlic cloves, minced
- 1 jalapeno pepper, seeded and finely diced
- 3 tablespoons fresh cilantro, finely chopped
- 1 lime, juiced
- ½ teaspoon sea salt

Instructions:

Place the avocado meat into a bowl together with the rest of the ingredients.

Stir until blended.

Serve immediately or keep it in your fridge until ready to use.

13. Cilantro and Mint Chutney

From Korea to India, here is a delicious chutney recipe that is meant to make fried pastries, also known as samosas, even more enjoyable. But no, that's not the only thing you can serve it with. The herby and fresh taste profile is also good with curries and other dishes.

Serving Size: 2 ½ cups

Preparation Time: 10 minutes

Ingredients:

- 1 hot green chili, stemmed
- 3 ½ cups cilantro leaves, finely chopped
- 1 cup mint leaves, finely chopped
- ¾ cup plain yogurt
- 3 tablespoons fresh lemon juice
- 3 tablespoons water
- Kosher salt to taste

Instructions:

Put all the ingredients in your blender or food processor, except for yogurt and salt, and pulse until smooth.

Fold in yogurt, sprinkle with salt to taste, and stir to blend.

Transfer chutney to a serving bowl or an airtight container and place in the fridge until ready to use.

14. Gravy

What's a mashed potato, steak, meatloaf, or kid's favorite fried chicken without a gravy? Boring, isn't it? This tasty sauce makes even the simplest recipes work wonderfully for everyone. And, it is so easy to make, even from scratch. You will not need more than 10 minutes until it's ready.

Serving Size: 1 cup

Preparation Time: 5 minutes

Ingredients:

- 1 beef bouillon cube, crumbled
- 1 chicken bouillon cube, crumbled
- 4 tablespoons unsalted butter
- 2 ¼ cups boiling water
- 4 tablespoons all-purpose flour
- ½ teaspoon onion powder
- Salt to taste
- ¼ teaspoon finely ground black pepper

Instructions:

Dissolve bouillon cubes into boiling water. Set aside.

Meanwhile, melt butter in your pan on medium fire and sprinkle flour to make a roux.

While stirring the butter and flour mixture, gradually pour the bouillon mixture until well blended.

Sprinkle with onion powder, salt, and pepper, constantly whisking until smooth and slightly thickened.

Serve with your meal and enjoy.

15. Tonkatsu Sauce

Pork Tonkatsu is a favorite meal not just in Japan but in the rest of the world as well. And the crispy on the outside but tender-juicy on the inside meat will not be as delightful without this sauce. So, we are giving you the recipe for the sauce to make sure you're at-home Tonkatsu experience is as authentic as it could be.

Serving Size: 1 ¼ cups

Preparation Time: 5 minutes

Ingredients:

- 1 teaspoon dry mustard powder
- ¼ cup Worcestershire sauce
- 1 cup ketchup
- 4 teaspoons soy sauce
- 2 teaspoons water

Instructions:

Dissolve mustard powder in water, then add the rest of the ingredients and whisk until well blended.

Transfer to an airtight bottle and refrigerate until ready to use.

16. Salsa Verde

Here is another Mexican sauce that is largely used for enchiladas and tacos. Apart from spreading it onto dishes, you can also use it as a dipping sauce for your chips, veggies and practically anything! As with other sauces, you can adjust the seasoning and level of spiciness. That's what makes the homemade sauce a tad more amazing!

Serving Size: 2 cups

Preparation Time: 40 minutes

Ingredients:

- 1 ¼ pounds tomatillos
- 1 white onion, quartered
- 4 serrano chilies
- 4 garlic cloves, peeled
- 12 cilantro sprigs
- 2 tablespoons vegetable oil
- Salt to taste

Instructions:

Place all the ingredients in your huge pan except for cilantro and salt.

Cover with enough water and heat on medium fire.

Boil, then simmer for 10 minutes. Set aside to cool a little.

Once mixture is cool enough to handle, transfer to a blender or food processor together with cilantro and pulse until smooth.

Meanwhile, heat oil in another pan and pour in the salsa. Let it simmer for the next 20 minutes until it is to your preferred consistency.

Sprinkle salt according to taste and stir.

17. Blue Cheese Dressing

If you want your family to go big on veggies, you should learn to make this blue cheese dip, which should keep them excited all the time. It is thick and creamy and would work with your cut-up veggies as well as your fried fish, chicken nuggets, and the like.

Serving Size: 3 cups

Preparation Time: 10 minutes

Ingredients:

- 4 ounces blue cheese, crumbled
- 2 cups mayonnaise
- 1 cup sour cream
- ¼ cup fresh parsley, minced
- 1 garlic clove, crushed
- ¼ cup white wine vinegar
- ½ teaspoon ground mustard
- ½ teaspoon salt
- ¼ teaspoon pepper

Instructions:

Put all your ingredients in the food processor or blender and pulse until smooth and creamy.

Store in your fridge 'til ready to use.

18. Garlic Aioli

Nothing beats a good old aioli. This is pretty simple and is almost like mayonnaise but with a significant kick. And for that simple addition of garlic into the recipe, everything changes amazingly. You can use it on your hot toasts, cold cuts, dressed seafood and more.

Serving Size: 1 8-oz jar

Preparation Time: 25 minutes

Ingredients:

- 2 egg yolks
- 1 cup extra virgin olive oil
- 3 cups olive oil
- 1 lemon, juiced
- 1 garlic clove, peeled
- Salt and pepper to taste

Instructions:

Whisk together the egg yolks and extra virgin olive oil.

Gradually, stir in olive oil and continue to whisk until the mixture thickens.

Add lemon juice and adjust seasoning.

Gently mash the garlic in a mortar and pestle together with a pinch of salt.

Stir garlic mixture into the egg yolk mixture.

Serve or place in a jar with a lid.

19. Marinara Sauce

Marinara sauce is another exciting sauce that will breathe a new life to your dining table whenever possible. It's a great dipping sauce for your bread, and it will also work well with your pasta and salads. It's great to have a jar of it in your fridge, ready anytime. And oh, before we forget, it tastes great with seafood, too. Bet you know that!

Serving Size: 2 cups

Preparation Time: 50 minutes

Ingredients:

- 1 28-ounce can whole peeled tomatoes
- 1 yellow onion, peeled and halved
- 2 garlic cloves, peeled
- 1 teaspoon dried oregano
- Pinch of red pepper flakes
- 2 tablespoons extra-virgin olive oil
- Salt to taste

Instructions:

Place all the ingredients in your saucepan and heat on medium fire, then turn the heat to low and cook in a simmer for about 45 minutes.

Stir the mixture occasionally, crushing the solids with the back of the spoon every once in a while.

Serve this at the dining table, warm, or store in an airtight container and chill to keep for at least 4 days. You may also freeze it, and it will be good for up to 6 months.

20. Chinese Style Sesame Sauce

This sauce is inspired by some Chinese restaurants. Made of broccoli and chicken and can be used as a dipping sauce for fried chicken or can be spread over fried chicken. A touch of vinegar is needed, but don't add too much so that it won't turn into a sweet and sour flavored sauce.

Serving Size: 1 cup

Preparation Time: 10 minutes

Ingredients:

- 1 cup white sugar
- 1/4 cup cornstarch
- 1 cup chicken broth
- 1/2 cup water
- 1/8 cup white vinegar
- 2 tablespoons dark soy sauce
- 2 tablespoons sesame oil
- 1 teaspoon chile paste
- 1 clove garlic, minced

Instructions:

Combine cornstarch and sugar in a saucepan.

Mix in water, sesame oil, garlic, chili paste, soy sauce, chicken broth, and vinegar.

Let it boil on medium heat while constantly stirring.

Reduce the heat and bring to simmer for 5 minutes.

21. Franks Style Hot Sauce

If you love hot sauce, you know about Frank's brand of sauce, let's teach you how to make it at home.

Serving Size: 1 cup

Preparation Time: 30 minutes

Ingredients:

- 18 Canned Cayenne peppers
- 1 ½ cups white vinegar
- 1 teaspoon garlic powder
- 1 teaspoon salt
- 1 clove of garlic

Instructions:

Roughly chop garlic.

Add all ingredients into your blender, then blend 'til smooth.

Add into a saucepan bring to a boil then reduce the heat and simmer for 20 minutes.

Let the mixture cool off then bottle it and put it in the fridge overnight before using.

Keep it in a bottle in your refrigerator.

22. Sweet Onion Sauce

This sweet sauce is savory and sweet at the same time and goes well with deli sandwiches.

Serving Size: 2 cups

Preparation Time: 20 minutes

Ingredients:

- 1/8 teaspoon poppy seeds
- ¼ teaspoon lemon juice
- 1 teaspoon dried buttermilk powder
- 1 teaspoon brown sugar
- 1 teaspoon balsamic vinegar
- 2 teaspoons white vinegar
- 1 tablespoon red wine vinegar
- 2 tablespoons onions
- ½ cup light corn syrup
- 1/8 teaspoon salt
- Pinch of black pepper
- Pinch of garlic powder

Instructions:

Dice onions very fine.

Combine all ingredients in a sauce and bring to a rapid boil.

Boil for 2-3 minutes constantly stirring mixture.

Turn off the heat and remove mixture.

Cool and enjoy.

Serve it immediately or you may keep it in an airtight container in the fridge.

23. Garlic and Chive Sauce

Great with grilled vegetables or meat, this sauce is creamy and fragrant and only uses ingredients that most people have in their pantry all year around. Nothing fancy, it is simple, but delicious.

Serving Size: 1 cup

Preparation Time: 5 minutes

Ingredients:

- 1/4 cup sour cream
- 1/4 cup mayonnaise
- 4 garlic cloves, minced
- 2 tablespoons chopped chives
- salt, pepper

Instructions:

Whisk together all ingredients in your bowl.

Season with your salt & pepper according to taste and serve right away for best taste.

24. Mint and Peanut Thick Sauce

Having Indian flavors, this sauce is great with curry or rice. Its flavors are intense, but not at all overpowering and the sauce is thick and creamy, perfect to dip some fresh bread in it.

Serving Size: 1 cup

Preparation Time: 10 minutes

Ingredients:

- 1/2 cup peanuts
- 1/2 cup packed mint leaves
- 2 green onions, chopped
- 3 green chilies
- 1 teaspoon tamarind paste
- 2 tablespoons vegetable oil
- 1/2 teaspoon mustard seeds
- 1/2 teaspoon cumin seeds
- salt, pepper

Instructions:

Put the peanuts in a pan and roast them in the oven until slightly golden brown.

Heat the olive oil in your heavy skillet and sauté the onion and chopped green chilies for 3-4 minutes on low heat. Stir in the mint leaves and cook 3-4 more minutes. Put this mixture into a blender. Add the tamarind paste and a pinch of salt and process until smooth. Transfer into a bowl and set aside.

Heat 1 more tablespoon of oil in another pan and stir in the mustard and cumin seeds. Cook them until they start popping and releasing their flavor. Pour this mixture in the bowl over the sauce and mix until well combined.

Serve it immediately or you may keep it in an airtight container in the fridge up to 4 days.

25. Asian Garlic Sauce

Easy to make, this sauce is great for Asian-inspired dishes but also served as it is on slightly cooked vegetables, such as broccoli or cabbage.

Serving Size: 1 cup

Preparation Time: 5 minutes

Ingredients:

- 4 garlic cloves, minced
- 2 teaspoons soy sauce
- 2 tablespoons sesame oil
- 1/2 teaspoon honey
- salt, pepper

Instructions:

. Mix all ingredients in your bowl and season with salt and pepper to taste.

To serve, dip the vegetables in the sauce or pour the sauce over them and toss to evenly coat them.

26. Balsamic Vinaigrette

This tangy sauce may be simple, but you cannot undermine its flavor. It can perk up your salads incredibly with its full-bodied flavor. Use it also as a dipping sauce for your sourdough and rolls. And the best thing about it? It's no fuss. You can prepare it in a jiff about 5 minutes. Yes, it's easy too!

Serving Size: 1 cup

Preparation Time: 5 minutes

Ingredients:

- 2 tablespoons honey
- ¼ cup balsamic vinegar
- ¼ cup extra virgin olive oil
- ½ teaspoon dried thyme
- 2 teaspoons Dijon mustard
- 1 garlic clove, minced
- Salt and pepper to taste

Instructions:

Place all your ingredients in a jar, cover with a lid, and shake vigorously until well combined.

Taste and adjust seasoning to your preference.

Keep it refrigerated and shake before using.

27. Salted Caramel Sauce

Great for your cakes and pies and even for your tasty drinks. Keeping a jar of the multi-purpose sweet sauce is witty for the days when you want to please yourself or impress others.

Serving Size: 1 cup

Preparation Time: 10 minutes

Ingredients:

- 6 tablespoons salted butter, at room temperature
- ½ cup heavy cream, at room temperature
- 1 cup granulated sugar
- 1 teaspoon salt

Instructions:

Heat sugar in a nonstick pan on medium-low fire, stirring with a wooden spoon until it becomes syrupy.

Whisk in butter and continue stirring for about 3 minutes.

Gradually add the cream and salt. Boil for around one minute, then turn off the fire.

Let it cool down before transferring to a jar and before using.

28. Maple Dijon Sauce

Sweet and sour, this sauce is probably one of the easiest to make. Combining just 3 ingredients, it is surprisingly delicious, and it will bring your meals to life. It works great with grilled meat or in sandwiches or on anything you think it might be suited for.

Serving Size: 1 cup

Preparation Time: 5 minutes

Ingredients:

- 3 tablespoons maple syrup
- 3 tablespoons Dijon mustard
- 2 tablespoons brown sugar

Instructions:

Put all ingredients in your bowl and mix until well combined.

Serve right away or you may keep it an airtight container in the fridge for up to 1 week.

29. Spicy Watermelon and Papaya Salsa

This salsa packs up all the flavors of summer, being light, fresh and simply delicious. The recipe is very easy to make, and it complements well seafood and fish.

Serving Size: 1 cup

Preparation Time: 5 minutes

Ingredients:

- 2 cups watermelon, deseeded and diced
- 1 small red onion, finely chopped
- 1 cucumber, peeled and diced
- 1 papaya, peeled and diced
- 1 tomato, peeled, deseeded and diced
- 2 red peppers, finely chopped
- 1/4 cup packed coriander leaves, chopped
- juice from 1 lime
- salt, pepper

Instructions:

Combine the watermelon, papaya, cucumber, tomato and red peppers in a bowl.

Add the coriander leaves and lime juice and adjust the taste with salt and freshly ground pepper.

Serve immediately or keep it in a jar in the fridge for 2-3 days.

30. Baba Ghanoush

This recipe has Moroccan roots and that only means that it is full of oriental flavors which makes it a perfect match for grilled meat or just served simple on toasted bread.

Serving Size: 2 cups

Preparation Time: 50 minutes

Ingredients:

- 2 eggplants
- 4 garlic cloves
- 1/2 teaspoon cumin powder
- 1 red pepper
- 1 tablespoon fresh chopped mint leaves
- 2 tablespoons olive oil
- salt, pepper

Instructions:

Arrange the eggplants and pepper on a baking tray and cook them on the oven at high temperature for 40 minutes.

Remove them from oven and when chilled, peel off the skin and remove the seeds. Put the flesh in a blender and add the garlic, mint and cumin.

Pulse a few times 'til a smooth paste form. Season with salt & pepper (to taste) and store in an airtight container in the fridge for up to 4 days.

Conclusion

Well, there you have it!

Sauces and condiments make mealtime an even more amazing experience. And you have plenty of choices, from the simple ketchup, or hot sauce, to the more elaborate concoctions like salsa, balsamic vinaigrette, and garlic aioli. You can also mix and match, depending on your main dishes, and put different small bowls or jars of the family's favorite sauces so everyone can choose which to use and flavor up their plate.

I hope you enjoyed reading all 30 delicious sauces and condiment recipes that are perfect for any time of day.

So, what's next?

Try the different recipes and see which one will be your favorite!

Good luck and happy cooking!

Afterthought

Thank You!

What a year, huh? Life is always full of ups and downs, but let's just say the virus took us all by surprise. Fortunately, some of us found a new sense of comfort in-home cooking, which helped us keep our sanity—if only a little longer. All I wanted to say is thank you.

Thank you for letting me enter your kitchen and fill your days with tasty recipes, even if life is a little crazy right now. No matter what you're going through, things will be okay. Just remember to take life one recipe at a time. Even the worst of days can be turned around with a nice meal, as I'm sure you've come to find with my cookbooks. I know because cooking certainly helped me push through some of the hardest moments of my life.

Thus, I wanted to give back to you by asking what kind of content you'd like to see more of from me. Would you like to see a comfort food book? What about a quick dinner on a budget? Being on the other end of this book only means that it's important for me to continue connecting with you through the recipes I make, so this is me asking… What would you like to cook next? Your ideas could inspire my upcoming books!

Thanks,

Noah W.

Biography

Noah was always the one assaulting the cookie jar throughout the day for a quick snack from an early age. Over the years, his love of cookies turned into an unparalleled curiosity that led him to the kitchen in search of the best recipes. As he got older, he wasn't the one emptying the cookie jar as much as he was the one filling it with different cookies every week!

His friends and family loved all of his recipes so much that, soon, the whole neighborhood was placing orders for Noah's baked goods. It was a lot of hard work, but it helped him grow enough confidence to start his own baking business and pursue a degree in Pastry Arts!

When he's not making cookies, he's sharing them with all of his loved ones because "you can't deal with life when you're low on cookies." Still, he likes to keep his personal cookie jar well-stocked and enjoys an occasional cup of coffee with cookies with his fiancé and two dogs, Figaro and Oreo.

⟨XXXXXXXXXXXXXXXX⟩

Printed in Great Britain
by Amazon